SCIENCE SPOTLIGHT

FAKES AND FORGERIES

SCIENCE SPOTLIGHT

FAKES AND FORGERIES

IAN GRAHAM

RSVP

RAINTREE
STECK-VAUGHN
P U B L I S H E R S
The Steck-Vaughn Company

Austin, Texas

Published by Raintree Steck-Vaughn Publishers, an imprint of Steck-Vaughn Company

Editors: Su Swallow and Shirley Shalit
Designer: Neil Sayer
Production: Jenny Mulvanny
Electronic Production: Scott Melcer
Illustrations: Hardlines, Charlbury
               Graeme Chambers

Library of Congress Cataloging-in-Publication Data

Graham, Ian, 1953-
    Fakes and Forgeries / Ian Graham.
        p.   cm. — (Science spotlight)
    Includes index.
    ISBN 0-8114-3843-0
    1. Fraud in science — Juvenile literature.
    [1. Fraud in science.]   I. Title.   II. Series.
    Q175.37.G73   1995
    001.9—dc 20   94-13834
                                        CIP AC

Printed in Hong Kong
Bound in the United States
1 2 3 4 5 6 7 8 9 0 LB 99 98 97 96 95 94

ACKNOWLEDGMENTS

For permission to reproduce copyright material the authors and publishers gratefully acknowledge the following:

Cover (top) Robert Harding Picture Library (bottom) Civico Museo Storico, Como, Robert Harding Picture Library **Page 4** (top) ET Archive (bottom) The Bridgeman Art Library **page 5** (top) Tim Fisher, Life File (bottom) English Heritage Photographic Library **page 6** (top) John Reader, Science Photo Library (bottom) Natural History Museum **page 7** (bottom left) John Cancalosi, Bruce Coleman Ltd (bottom right) Mary Evans Picture Library **page 8** (top) Popperfoto (middle and bottom) Mary Evans Picture Library **page 9** (top) The Yale University Library (bottom) Popperfoto **page 10** (middle) Mary Evans Picture Library (bottom) David Birchall, Life File **page 11** (top) Robert Harding Picture Library (bottom) Popperfoto **page 12** (top) Fergus Smith, Life File (middle) Sinrad (bottom) Topham Picture Source **page 13** (left) Sinrad (right) Tom McHugh, Oxford Scientific Films **page 14** Mary Evans Picture Library (bottom) Gerald Cubitt, Bruce Coleman Ltd **page 15** (top) Popperfoto (bottom) Morten Strange, NHPA **page 16** (top) Peter Menzel, Science Photo Library (middle) Popperfoto **page 17** Mary Evans Picture Library **page 18** (top) David Parker, Science Photo Library (bottom) ANT, NHPA **page 19** Kim Taylor, Bruce Coleman Ltd **page 20** (top) Topham Picture Source (bottom) Illustrated London News (bottom inset) Robert Harding Picture Library **page 21** (bottom centre) Sinclair Stammers, Science Photo Library (bottom right) Illustrated London News **page 22** (top) English Heritage Photographic Library (left) Victoria and Albert Museum (right) National Gallery **page 23** Metropolitan Museum and Brookhaven National Laboratory, Science Photo Library **page 24** (left) Michael Holford (right) British Museum **page 25** (left) Geco UK, Science Photo Library (right) Andrew McClenaghan, Science Photo Library **page 26** Robert Harding Picture Library **page 27** Alexander Tsiaras, Science Photo Library **page 28** (top) English Heritage Photographic Library (bottom) British Museum **page 29** (top) Michael Holford (bottom) Mary Evans Picture Library **page 30** (top) Michael Holford (bottom) Chris Payne, Life File **page 31** (top) Eric Crichton, Bruce Coleman Ltd (bottom) Zefa Picture Library **page 32** (top) John Walsh, Science Photo Library (bottom) Robert Harding Picture Library **page 33** (left) Michael Holford (right) GeoScience Features Picture Library (bottom) Sinclair Stammers, Science Photo Library **page 34** (top) Royal Mint (bottom) Michael Holford **page 35** (top) Michael Holford (bottom left) LJ Hall, Life File (bottom right) Mary Evans Picture Library **page 36** (top) Orville Andrews, Science Photo Library (bottom) Tim Fisher, Life File **page 37** Lawrence Livermore National Laboratory, University of California, Science Photo Library **page 38** Michael Holford **page 39** (top and bottom left) Michael Holford (bottom right) James Holmes, Oxford Centre for Molecular Sciences, Science Photo Library **page 40** Michael Holford **page 41** (left) John Reader, Science Photo Library (right) Robert Harding Picture Library **page 42** (top) Patrick Clement, Bruce Coleman Ltd (bottom) Brian Hawkes, NHPA **page 43** (top) Michael Holford (bottom) Robert Harding Picture Library

CONTENTS

INTRODUCTION

A fake is something that is not genuine. A forgery is a copy of something, especially a document, often made with the intention of cheating someone. This book reveals some of the ways in which scientists investigate suspicious objects and test just how genuine they are.

A 1930s watch decorated with imitation gemstones made from a hard, shiny glass called paste.

A picture in the style of Michelangelo by Tom Keating, a 20th-century art forger who copied many artists' work before a journalist uncovered the truth.

Fakes and forgeries have been made for thousands of years and for a variety of reasons. Some were made by artists learning how to produce fine paintings and sculptures by studying the methods of the great artists of the past. Most of these copies were not intended to fool anyone. But many of the fakes and forgeries made in past centuries were made to satisfy the demand for valuable or rare objects. When people believed that something worn or owned by a saint could perform miracles, these religious relics were highly sought after. So, forgers met the demand by producing fake relics. When a particular artist became popular, fakes painted in his style would find their way into the art market. This century, fine perfumes, designer clothes, and expensive jewelry are highly prized and so they have been the forger's most recent favorites. At other times, fake maps, musical scores, and diaries by famous people have also been produced.

EXPOSING FAKERY

Very often, fakes can be detected without the need for any sort of sophisticated scientific analysis. The trained eye of an expert in antique furniture, for example, can see through many fakes. Even if the style of a piece of furniture is faked perfectly, the wrong type of wood, nails, hinges, or varnish may have been used. The varnish may not show the natural wear that comes from several lifetimes of use, although

These are the genuine article, but copies of famous fashion items are common.

Objects dug out of the ground, even including bones, have sometimes turned out to be part of an elaborate hoax. Science can help to establish whether exciting finds are genuine or not.

furniture fakers are often expert at copying even this by a technique known as "distressing." Art experts often detect fake pictures by spotting errors in the way they have been painted – the style, the brushwork, or range of colors. But there are many other cases where science is needed to detect fakes that have succeeded in fooling the unaided eye. Science and technology give scientists more and more ways of detecting fakes and forgeries, but they are double-edged swords – they also give the forger new ways of making forgeries. Fortunately, scientists are usually able to stay one step ahead of the forger.

It is not always easy to decide whether something is a deliberate fake or forgery. A counterfeit $10 dollar bill is certainly a forgery and modern copies of prehistoric remains are fakes, but are crop circles (see pages 18-19) fakes? Are they all the work of practical jokers or a genuine freak effect of nature? Is everyone who claims to have seen the Loch Ness monster or a UFO mistaken? Or is a clever hoaxer at work? When is it not fakery at all, but the result of a genuine mistake or misunderstanding? Science cannot answer all the questions, but it can detect many deliberate fakes and forgeries.

Fakes and Forgeries looks behind the laboratory door and reveals the techniques used by the scientists who try to outwit the fakers and forgers. **History Spotlight** features throughout the book focus on famous figures, events, and scientific techniques in the history of the detection of fakes and forgeries.

THE MAN WHO NEVER WAS

Charles Dawson (left), who in 1912 seemed to have found the missing link between apes and humans. (Inset) A tooth from the Piltdown Man.

Until the 1850s, it was widely believed that people and all the different species of animals were created separately, but in 1859 Charles Darwin published a book called *The Origin of Species* with a theory to explain why there are so many different species. If he was correct, humans and apes had developed over millions of years from a common ancestor. If so, many people felt, there must have been creatures between apes and humans. In 1912, evidence of this "missing link" seemed to have been found.

THE PILTDOWN HOAX

In December 1912 Charles Dawson, an amateur archaeologist, and Pierre Teilhard de Chardin, a Jesuit priest from France, unearthed a cranium (the top of a skull) at a gravel pit at Barkham Manor on Piltdown Common in Sussex, England. Dawson returned to the site with the Keeper of Geology at the Natural History Museum in London, and they found more fragments of the cranium and a jawbone that appeared to match the cranium. When the cranium and jawbone were put together, they made an extraordinary pair because the cranium appeared to be human while the jaw was apelike. Other bones, flint tools, and the remains of animals found in the same place suggested that the

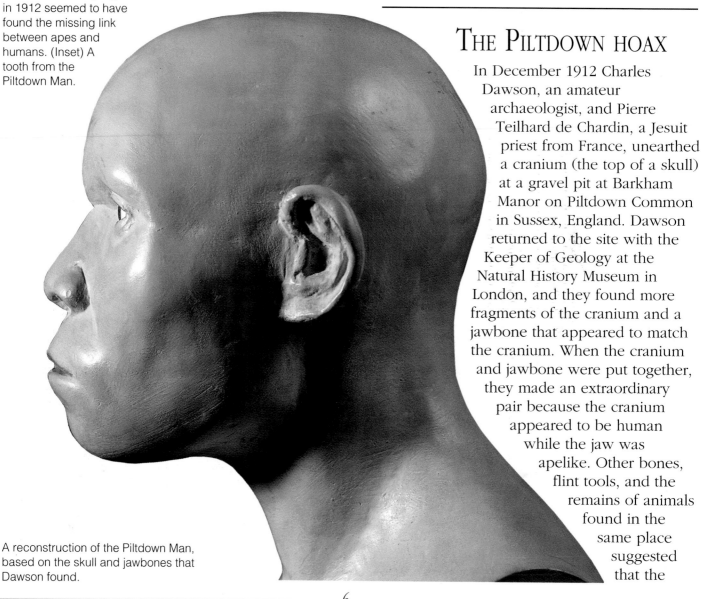

A reconstruction of the Piltdown Man, based on the skull and jawbones that Dawson found.

skull bones were about 200,000 years old. The skull of "Piltdown Man" was hailed as the proof the world was waiting for that Darwin's theory was correct. It appeared to be the missing link between apes and humans.

Most archaeologists accepted the finds as genuine. A few others had grave doubts about the original skull. Finally, the Keeper of Anthropology at the Natural History Museum in London, Kenneth Oakley, performed a test that cast doubt on the age of the Piltdown bones. The test relies on the fact that buried bones absorb the element fluorine from water in the ground. Bones that have lain in the same place for the same length of time should contain the same amount of fluorine. Oakley found that the Piltdown bones did not and therefore they could not all be the same age. The cranium contained much more fluorine than the jaw and so the cranium was much older. The jaw probably belonged to a modern ape called an orangutan. Its teeth had been filed down so that they looked more human and all the bones had been painted with potassium bichromate which stained them brown and made them all look very old.

The jawbones of the Piltdown Man were probably from an orangutan.

CALIFORNIA BONES

In 1876, human remains were found in gravel beds in Calevaras County, California, that had been dated to two million years ago. If the facts were correct, then these would be the oldest human remains found anywhere. In fact, the bones were those of local Native Americans which had recently been washed into the prehistoric gravel beds when a nearby river flooded. Miners at work in the gravel beds found the bones lying on the surface and took them to be examined by an archaeologist. The miners claimed the bones had been dug out of the gravel. But when a skull was examined, earth found inside it did not match the material in the gravel bed where it should have lain for millions of years.

HISTORY SPOTLIGHT

In 1922, a tooth was found in Nebraska, in earth dated to about one million years old. Specialists decided that it came from an ape-man and artists and modelers produced full-size paintings and figures to show what the whole ape-man would have looked like. In 1927, scientists returned to the site where the tooth had been found in the hope of finding more bones. As they brushed more earth away the skeleton emerged – not the skeleton of "Nebraska Man" but the fossilized skeleton of a prehistoric pig!

Nebraska Man turned out to be a genuine mistake. Piltdown Man, turned out to be a clever hoax. In both cases, artists produced reconstructions that were convincing – until science proved otherwise.

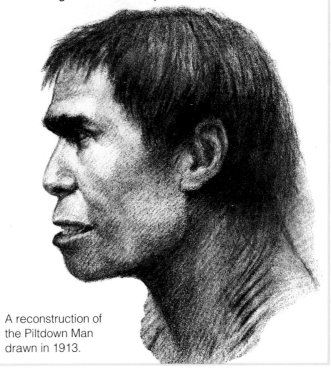

A reconstruction of the Piltdown Man drawn in 1913.

PAPER TRICKS

Rare maps, diaries, musical scores, manuscripts, and other documents can be forged to fool historians and collectors. Forged passports might help criminals escape and forged signatures trick bank tellers into handing over large sums of money. Fake documents are a serious problem and not always easy to detect.

An early instrument used to help detect alterations on documents.

Early maps are important documents because they show us how much our ancestors knew about the world around them. They show which seas they had crossed and which lands they had traveled to. But, like any document, a map can be forged.

The Italian seafarer Christopher Columbus (1451-1506) is usually credited as the first European to discover the "New World" of America. However, there have been many stories that other people, including the Vikings and the Irish, had reached America long before Columbus. In 1957, a map discovered in Switzerland provided more evidence to support the Viking stories. It appeared to have been drawn in 1440, more than 50 years before Columbus's voyage. It included an outline of a land called Vinlandia Insula, where we now know America lies. The map, known as the Vinland Map, was examined by experts in ancient maps. Some thought it was genuine, but others were not convinced. In 1972, samples of ink were taken from the map and tested. A chemical analysis discovered a compound called titanium dioxide in the ink in a form that was not available until the 1920s. If the test results were accurate, then the map must be a forgery. However, 12 years later in 1984, a new technique called proton-induced X-ray analysis was available. This could be used on the map itself without taking samples. This test produced a different result for the chemical makeup of the ink. It found only a tiny trace of natural titanium dioxide. If this test result is correct, the Vinland Map could possibly be genuine, but further tests will be needed to prove it. This is one case where science has not yet provided the answer.

Christopher Columbus.

There is no doubt that the Vikings (right) reached America long before Columbus, but does the Vinland Map date from before Columbus or from only a few years ago?

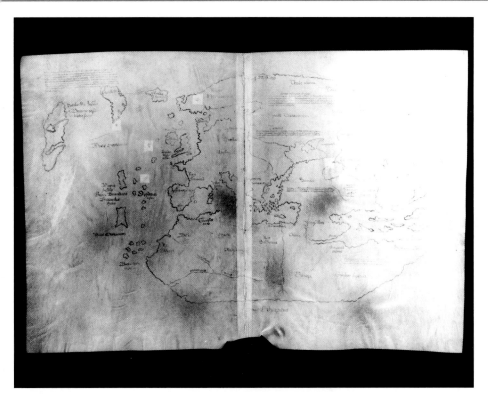

The Vinland Map, with Vinlandia Insula shown in the far northwest.

HITLER'S DIARIES

In April 1983 one of the biggest media scandals in recent history broke out when newspapers in Europe and the U.S.A. published what they thought were the diaries of Adolf Hitler. Hitler was the president of the Nazi Party in Germany between 1921 and 1945, so the discovery of such diaries would have been of huge historical importance.

For a short time, the diaries were a convincing hoax. It was claimed they had been rescued from a burning German aircraft at the end of World War II, and later "rediscovered" by a German journalist.

He persuaded his bosses at *Stern* magazine that the diaries were authentic, and they bought them for about $13 million. Other newspapers took up the story, including *The Sunday Times* in London, *Paris Match* in France, and *Newsweek* in the U.S. All of these newspapers, including *Stern*, ran features on the diaries. But the story broke before the diaries had been thoroughly investigated to see whether or not they were real. One historian who saw the diaries before they were published stated that they were indeed genuine. Yet only two days later he admitted that they could be forged. By this time the diaries had been read all over the world.

Public interest became so great that in May the diaries

A reporter holds up books which the German *Stern* magazine claimed were Adolf Hitler's personal diaries.

Handwriting analysis, or graphology, may be used to help identify the source of suspect documents, but it is not an exact science. In the early days of graphology, mistakes were made. In 1894 a French Army officer, Alfred Dreyfus, was accused of spying for Germany. His guilt or innocence depended on whether or not he had written a letter containing details of secrets passed to Germany. Alphonse Bertillon (a French detective) compared the handwriting in the letter to a sample of Dreyfus's handwriting and declared that Dreyfus had indeed written the letter. Dreyfus was court-martialed (tried by a military court), found guilty, and sent to Devil's Island, a convict settlement off the coast of French Guiana in South America. He was granted a new trial in 1899 but found guilty again. Finally, the Court of Appeals found him innocent of all charges in 1906. Bertillon had been incorrect – Dreyfus had not written the incriminating letter.

Dreyfus on trial for treason.

were submitted to the United Kingdom's Federal Archives for investigation. It took them only 48 hours to announce the diaries were fake. Signatures did not match originals, and chemical analysis showed that the paper, ink, glue, and binding were all manufactured after the war.

Two years of investigation followed in which it was discovered that the diaries had been forged by a dealer in Nazi memorabilia. Both he and the *Stern* journalist were sentenced to more than four years' imprisonment, and the reputations of newspapers involved in the hoax were badly damaged.

PAPER SECURITY

The widespread availability of high-quality color photocopiers and laser printers has made document forgery easier than ever.

These machines, which are found in most offices nowadays, can produce copies that are almost indistinguishable from the original document. One answer is to make the document from special paper that the forger cannot obtain easily. That is why some paper money is made from paper with a watermark and a metal thread running through it (see page 35). Watermarks have become very sophisticated nowadays. Paper can be made with a continuous watermark pattern all over the paper. Paper manufacturers are continually coming up with new and more ingenious "paper security" so that it is more difficult to make convincing forgeries and so that any forgeries that are made are also much easier to detect.

Colored fibers can be mixed with the pulp used to make paper. The paper is difficult for a forger to make, but colored fibers could be simulated by printing them on plain paper or by making color photocopies of the original paper. The manufacturers combat this by making their colored fibers from a synthetic material that is stronger than the paper itself. The fibers do not tear with the paper and so they can be seen poking out along the torn edge of the paper. Printed and photocopied fake fibers behave differently – they tear with the paper. This type of paper is very good for tickets or passes, where the ticket is torn off a stub as someone enters a building, an exhibition, or a sports arena. One clever variation on this is to incorporate fibers in the paper that look white in normal light but glow in bright colors when viewed in ultraviolet light. So the paper does not appear to be anything special until it is

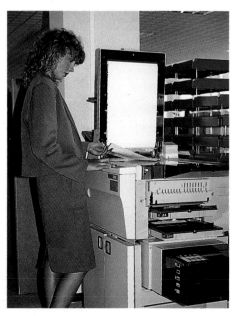

Photocopiers can now copy documents so well that the copies often look just like the original documents.

checked by passing it under an ultraviolet light. The paper may contain tiny disks called planchettes which can be made in any color. They can also be made from materials that look one color in daylight and a different color in UV light.

Paper can be impregnated with a variety of chemicals as a security measure. For example, it may be vital to protect handwriting on a document from being altered. One way a criminal may try to do this is by using a liquid called an ink eradicator, to bleach out the original name on a check or a contract and then writing in a new name. Paper used to make blank checks and other documents can be impregnated with a chemical that reacts with ink eradicator to show that it has been used.

The importance of paper in document security means that it is important to protect the paper itself from theft. Paper production plants are now

Paper can now be made with its own inbuilt security system to prevent forgeries.

highly secure buildings with video cameras monitoring all the work that goes on inside them.

One way of protecting documents that have to be stamped or signed to verify

them or cancel them is to split the ink used in the verification stamps and pens into two parts. The paper is impregnated with one part of the ink, an invisible chemical. The other part of the ink is used in the pen or rubber stamp that will be used on the document. If the correct stamp is used on the correct document, the two parts of the ink react with each other and the impression the stamp leaves is the correct color. If a fake stamp is used on a genuine document or a genuine stamp is used on a fake document, the resulting impression is a completely different color and the fake is immediately exposed.

A detective looking at a forger's equipment of the 1950s. The forger was caught because his money was printed with the 8s upside down!

A contour map of Loch Ness, based on readings taken before 1920 with a lead weight on a wire.

One study of the Loch Ness mystery is named after Urquhart Castle, which overlooks the loch.

A 3-dimensional image of one part of the loch, based on new data collected by sonar.

LOCH NESS MONSTER

For centuries, people have claimed to have seen extraordinary animals. Seafarers returned to their home ports with stories of mermaids and giant sea serpents. Most of these tales are now known to have been the result of myths, misunderstandings, exaggeration, and deliberate fakes. But some of them persist to the present day.

Fact or fake? An image of a long-necked animal in the waters of Loch Ness.

Loch Ness, Britain's largest freshwater lake, stretches over 21 miles (36 km) along a valley in northwest Scotland. People have reported sightings of strange creatures in its waters for almost 1,500 years. Some people have photographed strange water movements in the loch which they claim to have been caused by a large animal swimming at the surface or just below the surface. Others say that the water movements have nothing to do with mysterious creatures, but are due to the effects of wind, water currents, and the wakes of boats on the loch's surface. Some sightings have been put down to floating logs and vegetation. Bales of hay covered with tarpaulin were once floated on the water to look like the humps of a serpent swimming along. An umbrella stand made from a hippopotamus's foot was pressed into the soft earth around the loch to make a trail of fake footprints. And the body of an elephant seal was used to try to fool the monster hunters. But that still leaves a number of sightings, films, photographs, and curious readings from scientific instruments that cannot be explained.

Those who believe that a creature does live in the loch are divided as to what sort of creature it might be. Some think it is a giant eel. Others believe it is a creature that has survived from the age of the dinosaurs.

Most of Loch Ness's visiting monster hunters have tried to find the creature by scanning the loch's surface with binoculars and cameras. In 1960, a man filmed what looked like a large creature swimming along. His film was analyzed by experts, who described the object shown in the film as "probably animate" – that is, they believed it probably was a living animal of some sort. They estimated its size as up to 16.5 feet (5 m) and 6.6 feet (2 m) wide.

SEEING WITH SOUND

Other investigators have probed beneath the water's surface with sonar equipment. Sonar probes through the water and can detect anything moving around in it. It works by sending out bursts of high-frequency sound into the water and looking for any reflections that bounce back from solid objects. The latest scientific study of the loch, called Project Urquhart (named after a ruined castle on the loch's shore), began studying the

loch and its animal life in 1992. In addition to sonar, the project team also used sophisticated military equipment normally used to locate underwater mines. One day, the scientists detected a large moving object at a depth of 33 to 66 feet (10 to 20 m) and maintained contact with it for about two minutes. Some people believe it was yet more evidence for the existence of a large creature in the loch. Others believe the sonar trace could have been caused by a shoal of fish or even by water masses of different temperatures. Unless the whole creature can be filmed moving around clearly or the body of one of them is washed up on the loch shore, we may never know what, if anything, the creature that has become known as the "Loch Ness monster" really is.

HISTORY ◢ SPOTLIGHT

It may seem impossible for a prehistoric creature to have survived for so long when all the dinosaurs had died out, but creatures dating from those prehistoric times are not so unusual. Crocodiles, for example, have not changed much in millions of years. The first flying creatures on earth were dragonflies similar to modern dragonflies. In 1938, a fish caught 3 miles (5 km) off the coast of South Africa was found to be a member of a species which everyone thought had died out 80 million years ago — the coelacanth. It was a large blue fish with white blotches on its body. It was 5 feet (1.5 m) long, and weighed 127.6 pounds (58 kg). Unlike other fish, it had a broad paddlelike tail and its fins had thick muscular bases like the limbs of a land animal. It was 14 years before another coelacanth was caught, this time 1,200 miles (2,000 km) to the north off the Comoro Islands. More than 130 have now been caught in the same small area around the Comoros and they have even been filmed underwater from a submersible craft.

Scientists at work in a survey ship on Loch Ness.

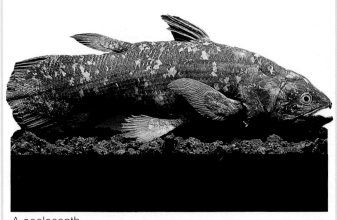

A coelacanth.

APE-MEN AND DRAGONS

There have been stories from several remote parts of the world of large humanlike apes and even modern dragons. At least one of them is true! Scientific proof for the existence of the others has not yet been found, but hoaxes have been uncovered.

This image appeared on the front page of a French weekly magazine in 1952, after Tibetan hunters reported seeing a terrifying manlike creature.

The Himalayas – home of the yeti?

About 300,000 years ago, our ancestors were not the only apelike creatures on earth. There was also a giant ape belonging to a different species thought to have stood 10 feet (3 m) tall and weigh over 550 pounds (250 kg). Hundreds of the creature's teeth and jawbones have been found, but, curiously, no other parts of its skeleton. Its height and weight are therefore guesses based on the huge size of the teeth and jawbones. It was called Gigantopithecus by scientists – meaning giant ape. Some people believe that the descendants of Gigantopithecus may have survived until the present day. It is possible that some of these creatures may be living in the icy foothills of the Himalayan mountain range. The creature, if it exists at all, is known to local people by the Tibetan word for snowman – yeti. It is also known as the abominable snowman.

Giant footprints in the snow, found in the Himalayas.

People have reported sightings of a giant humanlike ape covered with thick hair. Reports of giant footprints in the snow date back to the 1880s. During an expedition to the Himalayas in 1951, three mountaineers found a trail of huge footprints, each more than 12 inches (30 cm) long. Sir Edmund Hillary, who reached the top of Mount Everest in 1953, brought a scalp said to be a yeti scalp back from a Tibetan monastery he visited on a later expedition. But the "yeti" hair on the scalp was found to be goat antelope hair. The scalp was a fake.

BIGFOOT

Since the 1880s, there have been reports of another ape-man creature in the thick forests and mountains that cover much of northwest America. Its description seems remarkably similar to the yeti. Because of its large feet, this creature has become known as Bigfoot. In 1967 two men filmed what they described as a Bigfoot in an area called Bluff Creek in northern California. The film shows an apelike creature turning to face the camera and then loping away into the trees. Some experts say it is genuine, others say it is a hoax.

DRAGONS

One extraordinary animal tale has been confirmed. Early this century, there were stories of a dragon living on a remote Indonesian island called Komodo. The dragon was described as a giant animal that ate pigs and even people. In 1956, the British naturalist Sir David Attenborough went to look for the Komodo dragon. He found it and filmed it. The creatures he found were not the fire-breathing, flying dragons of fables. In fact, the island is home to a community of giant lizards that grow up to ten feet (3 m) long.

A komodo dragon.

FAKE FLIERS

M any people have reported seeing strange flying objects in the skies. Are all the sightings a result of natural phenomena such as cloud shapes and glowing planets? Or is the earth being visited by beings from another world? Have any of the reports and photographs been faked? Scientific analysis can explain some, if not all, the sightings and can help to find some of the fakes.

UFOs are sometimes tracked by air traffic control, and military aircraft can be guided to investigate.

Clouds can be mistaken for UFOs.

There have been thousands upon thousands of reported sightings of unidentified flying objects (UFOs). Astronomers and meteorologists (weather scientists) can often provide an explanation for these sightings. The planet Venus sometimes appears as a large bright ball in the sky and so it is often mistaken for a glowing craft of some sort. Strange formations of clouds gliding through the air together can be mistaken for solid flying objects. Weather balloons are another frequent source of UFO reports. Glowing insects called fireflies, airliners, and even satellites orbiting the earth can produce mysterious moving lights in the night sky. Airline flight plans, air traffic control records, and military flight logs can often show whether or not aircraft are the source of the sighting.

There still remains a small number, perhaps five percent, of sightings that cannot be explained away. What are they?

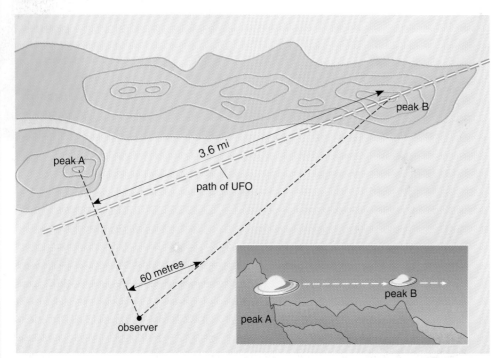

Films are more difficult to fake than photographs because they show how an object moves. If a film shows a UFO flying past two fixed landmarks (inset), the distance it covers can be measured from the film. The speed is calculated by dividing the distance by the time. The speed and distance are vital clues to the real identity of any UFO.

UFO hoaxers have filmed frisbees, and even a car's hubcap and claimed they were large spaceships flying hundreds of feet up in the air. But by comparing the focus of the UFO and the background, analysts can work out the size of the object and the distance from the camera.

peak B

3.6 mi

peak A

path of UFO

60 metres

peak B

peak A

observer

A hoax UFO may appear to travel 3.6 mi (6 km), but in fact covers only 66 yd (60 m).

Scientists think it is unlikely that we are the only living creatures in the universe. Our own galaxy, the Milky Way, contains roughly 200 billion stars similar to our sun. It is possible that at least some of them have planets similar to the Earth circling around them. And at least some of those earthlike planets may have given rise to life of some sort. But although scientists have tried to detect intelligent beings elsewhere by trying to pick up their radio signals, no evidence for their existence has been found yet. The latest SETI (Search for Extra-Terrestrial Intelligence) project began in the United States in October 1992, using the most sophisticated equipment yet used for this work. NASA's computers will analyze radio signals received from space faster than ever before. If anything other than natural radio energy from stars is detected, the system will immediately pinpoint its origin.

The Cottingley fairy photographs were first published by Sir Arthur Conan Doyle, who wrote the Sherlock Holmes stories. He, and many others, believed the photographs were genuine.

FAIRY PHOTOGRAPHS

In 1917 two young girls, cousins who lived in the Yorkshire village of Cottingley, England, produced photographs of the most extraordinary flying objects that kept the world guessing for more than 50 years. The flying objects in this case were fairies. Elsie Wright (15) and Frances Griffiths (9) claimed to have played with fairies in their garden. They took photographs of each other with the fairies dancing around them. Opinions were divided as to whether or not the photographs were genuine. Photographic analysis of the photographs was inconclusive. The puzzle of the Cottingley fairies continued until 1983 when the girls, who were by then elderly ladies, revealed that the photographs were fakes. The "fairies" were actually cutout paper figures held in place by hatpins.

CROP CIRCLES

Strange circles of flattened wheat have been appearing in farmers' fields for more than 300 years. Lightning, UFOs, animals, fairies, the hole in the ozone layer, and even the devil have all been blamed for making these strange circular patterns. Some of them have certainly been the work of hoaxers.

Strange patterns in a field of wheat.

Is the Wind Responsible?

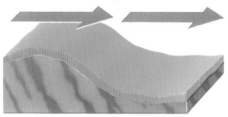

One theory claims that crop circles can be the work of the wind.

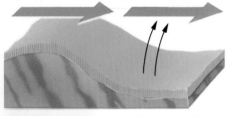

The wind begins to suck air up from the ground. In the right conditions, the rising air forms a tight column.

If air enters the base of the column faster than it can escape at the top, a bulge of air forms which circulates up and down.

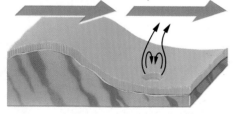

If the downward blast of air reaches the ground (because the bulge has descended the column) a circle of wheat is flattened.

Anyone who lives near wheat fields knows that tall ripening wheat can look like a golden sea as the wind bends the tall stems into rolling waves. But it can also be flattened by a downpour of rain as the weight of water and the force of the wind buckle the stems. Normally, the flattening is chaotic. It does not form any recognizable pattern. Crop circles, however, are quite different. The patterns of circles and lines are so precise that they look as if an intelligent being must have designed them. This strange phenomenon has been found all over the world, from England and the United States to Australia and Japan.

Some meteorologists believe that the effect may be caused by strong winds rushing over the brow of a hill, meeting a wall of stationary air on the other side and spiraling down to the ground. The spinning column of air flattens a circle of wheat as it rushes down onto the ground.

Is lightning to blame?

Some Japanese researchers believe that a substance called plasma is to blame. When air is heated by a flame or an electric spark, the energy of the flame or spark is enough to split its atoms apart into electrically-charged particles called ions. Air in this changed state is known as plasma. Lightning can turn the air around it into plasma. But if clouds of plasma are responsible for creating crop circles, a process that we do not yet understand must be at work. Japanese scientists have simulated the effect of a cloud of plasma on a wheat field by creating a small plasma cloud in the laboratory and allowing it to touch a plate covered by powder. The interaction between the two produced a complex pattern of circles and rings just like the pattern of a crop circle.

But what if wheat circles are simply the work of people walking around in circles flattening the wheat with nothing more than foot power? Two

British men claimed to have made most of the wheat circles found in previous years. Their work did fool some experts, but could they really have faked wheat circles for years undetected? They could not possibly have been at work in several different countries for up to 300 years! Have all crop circles in all that time been the work of hoaxers, or is some natural phenomenon at work?

CLEVER CAMERAS

The problem for scientists trying to investigate crop circles is that a circle of wheat flattened by feet looks much the same as a circle of wheat flattened by the wind or by a plasma. But science and technology can also help to catch the hoaxers. If crop circles are indeed made by people, they are probably made under the cover of darkness. Thermal cameras can see in conditions where the human eye sees only darkness. These cameras are sensitive to heat instead of light.

And human bodies are hot. Image intensifiers can also see through the night. They detect the tiny amounts of light reflected from objects, turn it into electricity and amplify it many times before changing it back to light again.

Thermal cameras and image intensifiers have been used to observe foxes, badgers, and other animals moving around at night. They are also used by military forces to detect the movements of troops and vehicles. They could certainly detect the activities of crop-circle hoaxers. The problem is that it is impossible to predict in which fields in which country the hoaxers will strike on any particular night.

As in the case of the Loch Ness monster, the yeti, and Bigfoot, a film of a crop circle forming could be the only way of solving the crop circle mystery, not only because we could all see it, but because scientists would have some evidence around which to build a theory.

Cameras normally used to photograph animals at night could be used to investigate the mystery of crop circles.

THE TURIN SHROUD

Detecting fake gems, coins, and statues is usually quite straightforward. The appropriate tests are carried out and the results point toward a forgery or the real thing. One object – a piece of linen – has been keeping everyone guessing for more than 640 years. Despite using the most sophisticated scientific tests available today, it still refuses to give up all of its secrets. It is the Turin Shroud.

The face on the Turin Shroud.

The shroud on view to the public in Turin in 1931. (Inset) Part of a replica of the shroud, showing the now faded image of Christ's face.

In about 1353, Geoffroy de Charny built a church in France and installed in it a piece of linen cloth 14 feet (4.25 m) long, which he claimed to be the shroud in which Jesus Christ was buried. It was therefore an extremely important article to Christians, if it was genuine. It bore the image of a man who, from marks on the body, appeared to have suffered the same injuries that the Bible says Jesus Christ suffered when he was crucified. There were many of these shrouds at that time, but most were clearly fakes with poorly painted images of Christ on them. The de Charny family's shroud appears to have been generally accepted as genuine from the moment it first was seen in public. In 1452, the shroud was presented to the Duke of Savoy (Savoy is now a region of southeast France). The duke had the shroud taken to Turin, the capital of his lands, in 1578. And there it has remained ever since.

The shroud has always had enthusiastic supporters who have believed it to be genuine, but others did not believe it to be the real thing. It was possible

that it was the same shroud that is reported to have been kept in Jerusalem and then Constantinople (now Istanbul, in Turkey) until the 13th century. Could scientific analysis provide the answer?

MODERN METHODS

The first application of modern technology to the shroud produced a surprise. The shroud was photographed for the first time in 1898. When the film was developed, the negative looked incredibly lifelike. The image on the shroud is actually in negative – parts of the face that are normally bright, like the nose, chin, and forehead, appear dark, and normally shadowed areas around the eyes and under the nose and mouth are lighter. If the shroud is a fake, it is remarkable that someone could have produced such an anatomically correct negative image of a human being at a time when paintings of people were not very lifelike and

human anatomy was not well understood. It is almost too remarkable to believe. If the image was indeed painted, there should be evidence of particles of paint trapped between the fibers of the cloth. But so far no such paint particles have been found.

Of course, if the shroud is genuine, it must be approximately 2,000 years old. When radiocarbon dating was developed (see pages 38 to 39), it held the promise of measuring the age of the shroud. However, the original radiocarbon dating method required large samples. About 64 square inches (400 sq cm) of the cloth would have been needed to produce enough carbon for the test. Too much material would have been cut from the shroud. But when a new small-sample method was developed in the 1970s, it was finally possible to apply the technique to this mysterious cloth. A few square centimeters of cloth (about 50 milligrams or one twentieth of a gram) was cut

from the shroud and shared between three laboratories in England (Oxford), Switzerland (Zurich), and the United States (Tucson, Arizona). The results of all the scientific testing indicated that the cloth was made somewhere between 1260 and 1390 – and the de Charny family first revealed the shroud to the world in about 1353. However, scientists still cannot explain how such a lifelike image of a man came to be on a piece of cloth of that age.

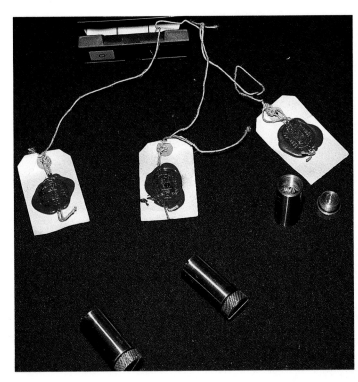

The containers in which tiny samples of cloth from the shroud were sent to different laboratories for testing.

HISTORY SPOTLIGHT

The Turin Shroud was examined by scientists in the 1930s, long before radiocarbon testing was available. First, the material was studied to establish that the image of a man had not merely been painted on the material. No trace of paint was found. Secondly, the anatomical detail in the image is quite beyond anything that was known and understood in the 14th century when the first records of the shroud appear. During a later analysis of the cloth, pollen grains from plants that grow around the Dead Sea were found. The imprints of coins over the eyes were identified as Roman coins dated to around A.D. 30, when Pontius Pilate still governed Palestine.

A 17th-century print showing the shroud in Turin.

THE GREAT MASTERS

Clever forgers can copy the style of a great artist, but it is more difficult for them to obtain the correct materials to paint with and on. Scientific analysis is often used to double-check that paintings are what they appear to be.

A conservation expert examining a painting under a microscope.

Everyone is familiar with the X rays used by hospital doctors to look inside a patient's body. The same technique can also be used to look beneath the surface of paintings. An X ray may reveal that an original painting has been altered by painting over all or part of it. Overpainting does not necessarily mean that the picture is a fake. Artists sometimes reused old canvases or changed a painting halfway through. So even when it is established that a drawing

A portrait of Edward VI of England, painted in the 17th century (left), and (below) the X-ray picture of the painting that lies hidden behind the young king.

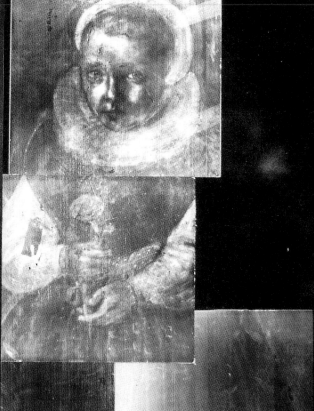

A painting by a 17th-century artist, Anthony Van Dyck.

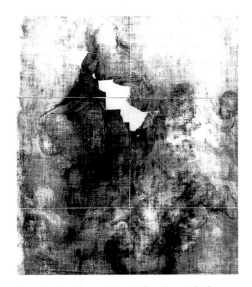

In a test using radioactivity, the painting was discovered to contain manganese, found in the yellow pigment umber. The test also revealed a hidden face – a self-portrait of the artist. Turn the page upside down to see it clearly.

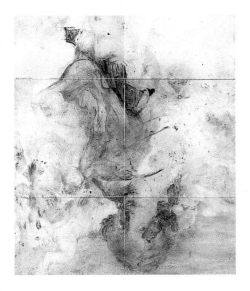

This image shows the presence of phosphorous, which is contained in charcoal. Van Dyck's self-portrait was sketched in charcoal and then overpainted. (Turn the page upside down to see the artist.)

or painting is a copy by one artist of an original by another artist, that does not necessarily mean that the copy was made with the intention of deceiving anyone. Artists frequently copy the work of other artists as a way of learning the techniques that more experienced artists have used.

CRACKS AND COLORS

Proving that a painting is a copy is one thing, but it is much more difficult to prove that it is a forgery. However, there are some things that genuine art students do not do. One of them is to fake the natural cracking that appears on the varnish on old paintings. In time, stresses and strains in the varnish make it crack. The random hairline cracks are difficult to simulate in forged paintings. Occasionally, art forgers have spent a long time painting fake cracks onto new varnish, but a close inspection with a good hand lens or a microscope should reveal the deception.

Artists often painted on wooden panels instead of canvas. If there are enough rings visible on the end of such a panel, it can be dated accurately using a technique called dendrochronology (see pages 42-43). One possibility is of course that a forger has obtained wood of the right age and made a modern painting

(see pages 42-43)

on it. He may try to make the forgery even more convincing by drilling fake woodworm holes through the painting into the wood. One way of exposing this sort of fraud is to analyze the pigments (coloring) in the paint. Just as the composition of metals has changed over the centuries, the chemical composition of pigments used by artists has changed through the ages. Some pigments used nowadays were simply not available to artists in previous centuries. If, for example, the green pigment used in a painting that is supposed to date from the 15th century turns out to be based on chromic oxide, the painting is a fake because chromic oxide green was not widely used by artists until the middle of the 19th century.

THE INSIDE STORY

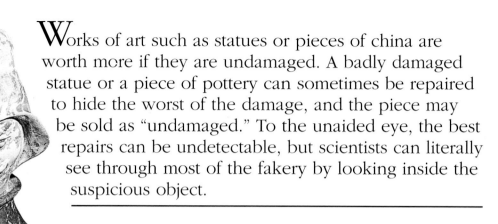

Rare statues like this early Chinese figure may easily get broken. Hidden repairs may be carried out by a museum for conservation – or by an unscrupulous dealer for profit.

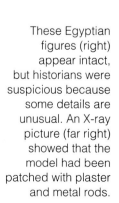

Works of art such as statues or pieces of china are worth more if they are undamaged. A badly damaged statue or a piece of pottery can sometimes be repaired to hide the worst of the damage, and the piece may be sold as "undamaged." To the unaided eye, the best repairs can be undetectable, but scientists can literally see through most of the fakery by looking inside the suspicious object.

Pieces of broken statues, figures, and pottery from the ancient world are quite easy to come by. Most have little value, but complete objects from the same period may be very valuable indeed to museums or private collectors. It is therefore very tempting for forgers to replace the missing parts of a statue or figure with plaster colored to match the original. It is even possible to stick pieces of completely different statues together to make a single statue. The faker may be able to match the color and texture of his plasterwork with the genuine statue, but he cannot fool an X-ray machine. If the object has been repaired, an X ray will reveal the patchwork of different materials. The softer plaster used for repairs is less dense than the original stone or pottery and X rays pass through the

These Egyptian figures (right) appear intact, but historians were suspicious because some details are unusual. An X-ray picture (far right) showed that the model had been patched with plaster and metal rods.

A chemist using an atomic absorption spectrometer to discover what metals are present in an unidentified sample.

A simple flame test can be used to identify elements. Copper burns with a green flame. Copper is found in bronze, an alloy often used for making statues, and in some ancient glass.

less dense areas of the object more easily. If several pieces of pottery have been put together to make a single object, the pieces may have been strengthened by mounting them on metal spikes or wire, which are then covered by plaster. X rays pass through the plaster but any metalwork inside the object blocks the rays and shows up clearly on the X ray. (Other tests that use X rays to investigate objects are described on pages 28 and 29.)

Techniques such as atomic absorption spectrophotometry (AAS) and inductively-coupled plasma spectrometry (ICPS) can also be used to test objects.

In AAS, a tiny sample of the suspect material is dissolved in acid and sprayed into a flame. Every element produces a characteristic flame color, but AAS goes further than this crude type of flame test. Light of the same color as the flame produced by one of the elements in the sample is shone through the flame. The atoms of that element not only give out light of that particular color, they can

also absorb it. So they absorb some of the light shining through the flame. The more atoms there are, the more light they absorb. So the intensity of the light after it has passed through the flame gives a measure of the amount of the element that is present. This is repeated for each element, so the scientist can build up a complete picture of the composition of the material.

ICPS is a much quicker test. A very hot flame called a plasma flame is used to turn the dissolved sample into vapor and the spectrum of colors produced by all the elements present in the sample is then registered by an electronic sensor, or it may be photographed.

TRACING MARBLE

Marble was a favorite stone with sculptors. Scientists can now test marble to find out where it was quarried. The test is called stable isotope analysis. Many elements exist in more than one form. Carbon and radiocarbon, for example, are two forms of the same element. Such elements are called isotopes. The difference between them is the number of neutrons in the nucleus at the center of the atom. Carbon and oxygen each exists in two stable forms in marble. Because they are stable, they do not change over the centuries. The ratio of one isotope to the other is the same throughout the quarry where the marble was dug out of the ground, but different from marble from other quarries. To test a statue, a small sample of the marble is crushed and dissolved in acid. The reaction gives off carbon dioxide gas, which is analyzed by a mass spectrometer to show how much of each isotope is present.

If a marble statue is claimed to be from ancient Greece, but the stable isotope test shows that the marble came from a quarry in Italy, it is very likely to be a fake, especially if no trade in marble between Italy and Greece (which had its own marble quarries) was known at the time. Fake statues made up from several pieces of marble from different places are also exposed by this test.

Techniques like X-ray fluorescence, X-ray diffraction (see pages 28-29), atomic absorption spectrophotometry, inductively-coupled plasma spectrometry, and stable isotope analysis make it virtually impossible for the forger to fool the scientist. However, some of these tests are extremely expensive to perform and so objects may only be tested if they have first been doubted by the experts.

AN ANCIENT EGYPTIAN GOES TO THE HOSPITAL

Egyptian mummies (the preserved bodies of ancient Egyptians) were wrapped in linen bandages and encased in a stone sarcophagus, or coffin. Unwrapping a mummy to examine the body inside is a long and difficult task, and the body can be damaged as the last bandages are removed. A modern technique called computerized axial tomography (CAT), normally used in hospitals to look inside living people, is sometimes used to

A marble quarry in Tuscany, Italy.

An Egyptian mummy moves into the CAT scanner. Inscriptions on the coffin identify the body as Ta-bes, a female singer in a temple in Karnak around 900 B.C.

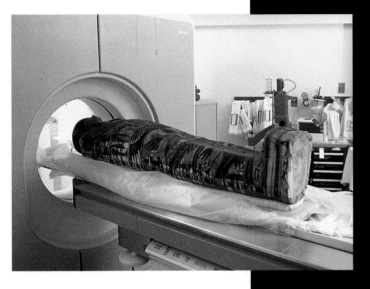

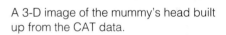

A 3-D image of the mummy's head built up from the CAT data.

A series of 3-D images of the mummy's skull.

HISTORY SPOTLIGHT

The computerized axial tomography (CAT) scanner was developed in the 1960s by the British electronics company EMI. The first scanner was made available to the medical profession in 1972. An X-ray tube was rotated around the patient's head, taking a series of X-ray images at different angles. When these were combined by a computer, it produced an image of a slice through the brain. The brain scanner was soon followed by a whole-body scanner, which works on the same principle. The patient lies on a motorized bed so that doctors can produce an image of a slice through any part of the body. It has proved invaluable for finding tumors (cancer growths) and monitoring the progress of treatment. Until the CAT scanner was developed, doctors had to operate on patients to find the source of a problem.

examine the mummy without unwrapping it. By taking X-ray images from different angles and combining them in a computer, the system can produce images of slices through a living patient, or a very dead mummy! Pictures like this can establish that the bandages really do contain a body without any need to unwrap it. It can also help historians to find out about the medical condition of the ancient bodies at the time of death.

MIMICKING METALS

A research scientist examines a copper alloy flagon.

Metals that are scarce or difficult to make have become the most valuable. Since ancient times, people have tried to fake the most valuable metals and the objects that are made from them.

Ever since people learned how to make metals about 10,000 years ago, they have used them to make tools, weapons, ornaments, and jewelery. Modern metals are often different from the ancient forms because of changes in the ways in which they are produced. These differences give scientists a way of checking the age of at least some suspicious metal objects.

Pure metals are often soft and unsuitable for making tools and weapons. People soon learned how to combine two or more pure metals together to make an alloy that was stronger than either of them. For example, the type of silver used to make everything from tea sets to watchcases, called sterling silver, has always contained a small amount of copper, because the addition of copper hardens the silver. Without it, the metal would bend too easily. Some alloys occur naturally. The

An X-ray test called X-ray fluorescence (XRF) was used (right) to test these figures. In XRF, a beam of X rays is pointed at an object. The material of the object interacts with the X rays and gives out a new group of X rays, which in turn reveal which material produced them.

XRF showed that the top figure was a genuine Etruscan bronze (copper with some tin and a little lead). The bottom figure is of brass (copper with some zinc). Brass was not used by early Etruscans so it is probably a modern fake.

silver used in ancient Rome, for example, always contained a little gold. If a silver object that is claimed to be from ancient Rome raises any suspicions, a test of the metal will reveal whether it is genuine or not.

X-ray fluorescence (see page 28) is often used to investigate metals and alloys. But if a pinhead-sized sample of the metal can be taken for analysis, a second technique called X-ray diffraction can detect even smaller traces of impurities. The technique relies on the fact that the atoms of a crystalline material like a metal are arranged in regular sheets and clumps. When a beam of X-rays is directed at a crystal, the atoms in the crystal deflect the beam.

X-ray Diffraction

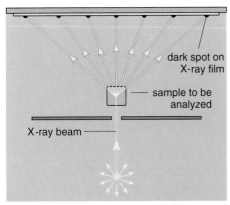

The atoms in the test sample deflect the X rays, which make dark spots on a piece of photographic film. By measuring the angles by which the beam has been deflected, scientists can work out the arrangement of atoms in the sample.

The information can also be shown as a trace on a screen, where each peak represents a deflected beam and its height represents the strength of the deflected beam. Each trace is characteristic of a particular crystal structure.

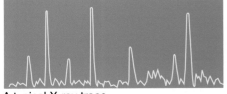

A typical X-ray trace.

The way the beam is deflected depends on the types of atoms present and the way they are arranged. When a beam of X rays shines through or bounces off a crystal, it produces an invisible pattern of spots that can be recorded on film just like a hospital X ray, or turned into a trace on a screen. Each type of metal produces its own individual "signature" in the form of a unique pattern of spots.

WIRE IN CLOSE-UP

Metal pots, statues, and ornaments are often finished off with intricate decorations made from fine wire. Modern wire is made by an entirely different method from ancient wire. The different wire-making techniques show up under a microscope. In ancient times, wire was made by one of two methods. A long and narrow strip of metal would be wound around to form a hollow tube. The spiraling edges of the original metal strip can be seen clearly under a microscope. The second method started with a long thin square-section rod which was twisted around and around and then rolled. This also has a spiral pattern which can be seen under a microscope. Modern wire is made in a different way. A metal rod is pulled through a series of plates called draw plates. Each draw plate has a smaller hole in it than the previous one, making the rod thinner and thinner, eventually turning it into wire many times longer than the rod. Under a microscope, modern "drawn" wire has marks running along its length instead of around it. Fake wire is therefore very easy to spot.

This Greek ornament dates from 600 B.C. A close inspection of the fine gold wire could help to confirm its age.

HISTORY SPOTLIGHT

The technique of X-ray diffraction was developed by William Henry Bragg (1862-1942) and his son at the beginning of the 20th century. Together, they worked out the laws of nature that govern the ways that crystals affect X rays. The result was Bragg's Law. They jointly received the Nobel Prize for Physics in 1915 for their pioneering work.

William Henry Bragg

TRANSPARENT FAKES

It is very difficult to fake glass convincingly because scientists have developed methods for analyzing glass and comparing the results with what archaeologists and historians know about how glass was made.

Glass is made from silica, commonly found as sand on the seashore. The sand is heated until it melts. The molten sand runs together and cools to form glass. However, glass has never been made from pure silica. It has always contained a mixture of materials that were added to make the glass easier to produce and longer lasting. By measuring how much of which materials are present in a piece of glass, scientists can sometimes estimate its age.

Pure silica melts at 3,092° F (1,700° C), but ancient glassmakers had no way of heating sand to such a high temperature. Their solution was to add impurities to the silica to lower its melting point. Soda and potash were the glassmaker's favorite impurities because they could be made easily by burning plants. Plants grown in salty water produce an ash rich in soda, potash, and another material called magnesia. By adding this plant ash to silica, glassmakers were able to lower its melting point to around 1,832° F (1,000° C). Lime was also added to the mixture to make the glass less prone to corroding and dissolving. So genuine ancient glass should contain silica, soda, potash, lime, and magnesia in certain quantities.

Around the seventh century, a new type of glass with a different chemical makeup appeared. Roman glassmakers found a different source of soda, a purer mineral called natron, found in dried lake beds. It contained much less potash and magnesia than glasses made with plant ash. This type of glass was

A Roman glass jug, found in Reims, France.

A glassblower heats a ball of glass over a wood fire.

used for about 200 years, and then, in about the ninth century, glassmakers returned to the old way of obtaining soda from plants.

Meanwhile, in Europe, glassmakers started making glass with ash made by burning wood. This contained less silica and much more magnesia, lime, and potash than the plant ash or natron glasses.

By glass, we usually mean clear colorless glass nowadays, but in ancient times clear glass was rare because the primitive glassmaking process tended to produce colored glass. The color came from impurities in the molten silica mixture. Glassmakers discovered ways of getting rid of this unwanted color by adding more chemicals to the mixture. An element called antimony was used for this until about 200 B.C., so clear glass made before this should contain some antimony. Clear glass made after this used another element called manganese to get rid of unwanted color.

Compounds of antimony could also be used to achieve the opposite effect – to make glass opaque. These opacifiers, as they are called, were made from antimony compounds until about the fourth century A.D., when they were replaced by tin compounds. Modern glass also contains more lead, and other elements such as arsenic and zinc, than ancient glass. So, if glass that is supposed to have come from ancient Egypt turns out to have a high lead content and possibly other elements such as arsenic, then it is probably a fake.

Glass was also used to make enamel by fusing it to metal.

In marshy areas, reeds were cut and burned to produce potash and magnesia for glassmaking.

Wells were made in the metal's surface, by soldering wire onto the metal surface or pressing depressions into it. The wells or depressions were filled with powdered glass. When this was heated, the powder melted to form glass. By using colored glasses, complex pictures or patterns could be produced.

Enameling was used to produce highly decorated goblets, urns, pictures, and ornaments. It is also possible to fuse colored glass onto clear glass, to decorate drinking goblets, for example. Enamels can be analyzed in the same way as glass to reveal their true origins, whatever they are claimed to be.

All these factors, and the different recipes that glassmakers have used through the centuries, make it very difficult for a forger to make a fake ancient glass that would fool a scientist.

HISTORY SPOTLIGHT

No one knows how, where, or when glass was made for the first time. But it is likely that glass was made for the first time about 4,500 years ago. It was probably made by accident when the fierce fires used to extract metals from their ores in the Bronze Age turned sand in the ore or on the ground around the fire into glassy beads. This probably happened many times before anyone noticed it and went on to try to make glass itself.

How was the link first made between sand and glass?

A GEM OF A FAKE

A sapphire seen under a microscope.

Gemstones are minerals that are rare enough to make them valuable, sought after for their beauty, and hard enough to last a lifetime. People have been copying gems for at least 6,000 years. The high value of some gemstones makes them a prime target for forgers.

Gemstones come from the Earth's crust and the layer below it, called the mantle. Some gems, diamonds for example, are formed deep underground where the conditions are just right – very high temperatures and enormous pressures. Others are formed higher up, closer to the surface, by reactions between lava (molten rock) and cooler solid rocks that contain metal ores. If lava meets rock rich in chromium, emeralds may be formed as the mixture cools down. Yet others, jadeite for example, form where the ocean crust rubs against the land, creating very high pressures. These gem-bearing rocks are brought to the surface when lava pushes upward through the crust or when vast volumes of crust are pushed upward when mountains are formed.

Natural gems are rough and dull. They only take on their brilliant, sparkling appearance when they are cut and polished. Flat surfaces, called facets, are often ground into the stone. The wear and tear on the facet edges may reveal a fake gem to the expert eye. The gem forger can work in one of three ways. He can use glass or cheap stones to imitate more valuable gems. Or he can make a "composite" fake from two different stones stuck together so that they look like a valuable gem. Finally, he can make a fake gem from a synthetic (man-made) material.

A jeweler inspects a diamond.

SHEDDING LIGHT ON FAKES

Light can be used to check gemstones. When a ray of light passes from air into a gemstone, it changes direction. You can see the same effect if you dip a straw into a glass of water. The straw looks bent. This effect is called refraction, and the amount by which the light is bent is given by a number called the refractive index. Each type of gem has its own refractive index that can be measured by a refractometer. If glass is used to imitate a gem, the refractometer will show that it has a refractive index of between 1.5 and 1.7. No gem has a refractive index as low as this.

An 11th-century book cover of gold set with precious stones and enamel work.

MAKING SYNTHETIC GEMS

Synthetics are artificial gems made in a laboratory. A molten bath of the chemicals found in the natural gem is allowed to cool under carefully controlled conditions. As the liquid cools, a crystal begins to form. The process continues until all the dissolved chemicals have crystallized out of the liquid to form one large synthetic crystal. Although the natural and synthetic gems are chemically identical, gems made in the laboratory grow in a different way from gems formed in nature, and the gem expert can usually see these differences. For example, under a microscope, a synthetic opal appears to be made from a honeycomb of minute cells that look like fish scales. And synthetic rubies have a characteristic pattern of growth that looks like the growth rings inside a tree trunk.

A mixture of natural and synthetic diamonds.

COUNTERFEIT MONEY

Newly-minted coins.

C oin makers and paper money printers have had to use more and more sophisticated minting and printing methods to foil the forgers.

In the early days of coinage, theft of the metal the coins were made from was at least as serious a problem as counterfeiting. Coins used to be worth the value of the metal that they were made from. Because the coins were made by hand, they were often misshapen or unevenly stamped and it was easy to clip tiny pieces of valuable metal from the edges without anyone noticing. Machinery had taken over coin production by the 17th century and made this practice more difficult to get away with. Machine-made coins were more uniformly circular, so it was harder to cut off pieces unnoticed. They also had a ridged edge called milling so that any edge-clipping was immediately obvious.

To spot fake coins, it helps to know when each metal or alloy was first used. For example, bronze (an alloy of mainly copper and tin) has changed in composition over the centuries since it was first made about 6,000 years ago. When aluminum was discovered and extracted in the 19th century, it was alloyed with bronze to form aluminum bronze. If coins appear to be 1,000 years old but are found to be made from aluminum bronze, then they must be fakes made in the 19th century or later.

A favorite method for making counterfeit coins in the ancient world was to cover a disk made from a low-value metal like copper with a thin skin of silver to make a coin that looked like solid silver. If these coins became worn at the edges, the copper core sometimes showed through. Gold coins could be faked in the same way – by a process called gilding (sticking paper-thin sheets of gold to the copper), or by dipping the copper in molten gold. If a coin is suspected of being a forgery, X-ray diffraction (see page 29) can be used to establish what it is made from. It is an ideal technique

A Roman silver coin from 44 B.C. Early coins were irregular in shape and it was not difficult to steal pieces of metal from the edges.

because it probes the coin's surface in great detail without the need to remove a sample of the metal.

PAPERING OVER THE CRACKS

Unscrupulous printers soon tried their hand at copying early paper money and they have been trying it ever since. In one month in 1993, detectives in Britain seized fake money and travelers' checks with a face value of more than $30 million. To combat the counterfeiters, banks worldwide have tried to make money more difficult to copy. They use special paper, impressed with watermarks that show up as light patterns on a darker background when the bill is held up to the light. The paper also sometimes has a metal strip running through it. The printing itself involves extremely intricate patterns that are very difficult to copy. The special inks used glow under ultraviolet light.

Up to a quarter of counterfeit paper money may be produced on color photocopiers. Although the fake bills may look real, they may feel shiny, whereas genuine bills should feel rough in places. One new photocopier is fitted with a device that prevents it copying some money, and ensures that it tags every copy it makes with an invisible code, which will allow detectives to trace fake money back to a particular copier. (See also pages 10 and 11.)

A gold Greek coin.

French money from 1793. Early paper money was much easier to copy than today's designs.

(See also pages 10 and 11.)

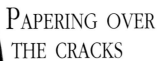

HISTORY SPOTLIGHT

When Hiero II, the ruler of Syracuse, gave a lump of gold to a jeweler to make him a crown, he suspected that the jeweler had kept some of the gold and made the crown from a mixture of gold and silver. He set Archimedes the task of testing the crown.

Gold weighs more than the same volume of silver, so a pure gold crown weighs more than a crown of the same size made from gold and silver. But weight alone will not reveal a fake, because a larger gold and silver crown would be the correct weight. Archimedes' problem was to measure not only the weight of the crown but also its volume. If he could do this, he could compare the weight and volume of the crown to the weight of a known volume of pure gold. The two weights should be identical. The answer came to him while he lay back in a full bath and saw the water overflowing. He shouted *Eureka*! He submerged the crown in a full tank of water and weighed the water that overflowed. Then he weighed the water displaced by an equal weight of gold and then an equal weight of silver. The weight of the water displaced by the crown was somewhere between the weight of water displaced by the pure gold and the pure silver, so the crown must have been made from a mixture of gold and silver. Hiero II had indeed been cheated!

Archimedes

Mirrors reflecting a laser beam.

3-D SECURITY

Fake copies of a huge variety of goods are made nowadays. They range from expensive watches and perfumes to leather goods and designer clothes. They are made because many of these goods are highly valued and much sought after. The copies are made using poor quality materials, so they can be sold at a much lower price than the genuine article. Science is rarely used to discover these fakes, but it is used to prevent some fakes being made in the first place.

In the 1980s, home video suddenly became very popular. Videocassettes of feature films were made by transferring the films onto magnetic recording tape. However, if a film or a tape of the film was available, it was very easy for someone to transfer this onto another videotape cassette or, if they had the appropriate equipment, onto hundreds or thousands of new videocassettes. So many counterfeit videos were made that lawful video companies lost millions of dollars worldwide. Counterfeit videocassettes became such a serious problem in the 1980s that the video industry set up security organizations to track down the sources of counterfeit videos. A few video distributors tried to tackle the problem at its source by making genuine videotapes as difficult as possible to copy. Although the tape itself was ordinary videotape, the plastic case, or shell, was made difficult to copy by adding a special type of picture called a hologram to it.

Most credit card companies and banks also print holograms on their credit cards and check guarantee cards to prevent them from being copied. Manufacturers of some fashion items are beginning to use holograms as decorative items, but not so far as a security measure.

Holograms are special because they appear to show a three-dimensional lifelike image on a flat sheet. If you move your head from side to side,

A close-up of a hologram on a credit card.

Laser equipment used to etch detailed hologram patterns being tested in the laboratory at the University of California.

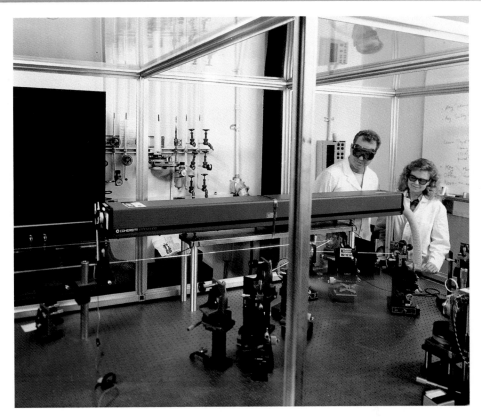

the picture changes. If you do the same with a normal picture or photograph, it stays the same. But if you do this with a hologram, you will find that you can look around things that appear to be closer to you and see the things behind that were hidden. It seems to be an impossible feat.

MAKING A HOLOGRAM

The flat sheet on which the hologram is recorded does not contain a picture in the normal sense. A holographic picture is made by pointing a laser beam at a photographic film. The object to be recorded is positioned next to the film. Laser light reaches the film in two ways. It strikes the film directly (this is called the reference beam) and it is reflected back onto the film from the object. The reference beam and the reflections meet on the film. Where the light waves are in step with each other, they reinforce each other to make a stronger light wave. Where they are exactly out of step with each other, they cancel each other out and there is no wave. And where they are only partly out of step, they will combine to form a wave part way between the two in strength. This pattern of light and dark, called an interference pattern, is recorded on the film.

The first holograms could only be viewed in the same laser light that was used to make them, but in the 1960s scientists learned how to make holograms that could be seen in normal daylight. And that has led to the 3-D holographic labeling that is used nowadays. Holograms hold one final surprise. If you break up or cut up a photograph or printed picture, each piece shows a small part of the whole picture. But if you break up a hologram, you will see the whole picture in each one of the pieces! The criminals who make fake credit cards and videocassettes do not have the technology necessary to make holographic labels ... yet!

HISTORY SPOTLIGHT

The Hungarian physicist Dennis Gabor (1900-1979) developed the theory of holography in the 1940s while he was working in Scotland. He made the first hologram in 1948. Early holograms were dim and blurred because there was not a sufficiently intense light source available with a property called coherence. Daylight and light from bulbs and fluorescent tubes contain all wavelengths (colors) of light and all the waves are out of step with each other. Holograms are best made with light that contains a single wavelength in which all the waves are lined up with each other, called coherent light. The invention of the laser by Theodore Maiman in 1960 provided a powerful source of coherent light. It enabled holography to progress much further. Gabor received the 1971 Nobel Prize for Physics for his achievements.

DATING BY DECAY

The ability to measure the age of an object would give scientists a way of detecting at least some fakes. If something that appeared to be, say, 1,500 years old was found to be only 500 years old, it could not possibly be genuine. Fortunately, scientists have developed several different methods for dating objects. The best known is probably radiocarbon dating.

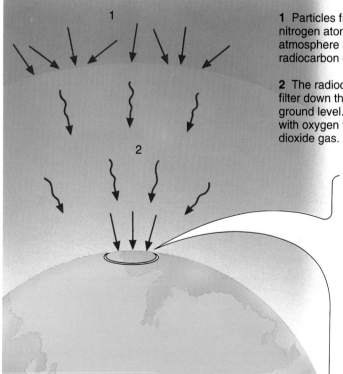

An archaeological dig. Objects can be dated to see if they belong to the site where they were found.

Most of the atoms that make up everything around us are stable. They do not change. An atom of aluminum, for example, will still be an atom of aluminum tomorrow, next year, or ten years from now. But some atoms are unstable. These "radioactive" forms of materials can suddenly change from one element to another by a process called radioactive decay. And they continue to decay until they reach a stable form. One form, or isotope, of the element carbon is unstable in this way. This radioactive form of carbon, called radiocarbon, can be used to discover how old some things are.

Radiocarbon is formed in the top of the Earth's atmosphere and passes eventually into plants and animals. (See diagram below.) When plants and animals die, they stop taking in radiocarbon. The radiocarbon that they already have in their body decays to form nitrogen again. As it decays, the amount of radiocarbon falls at a steady rate. After 5,730 years, half of the radiocarbon atoms will

1 Particles from outer space strike nitrogen atoms at the top of the Earth's atmosphere and change them into radiocarbon or carbon-14.

2 The radiocarbon atoms gradually filter down through the atmosphere to ground level. On the way they combine with oxygen to form radioactive carbon dioxide gas.

3 The carbon dioxide dissolves in the sea, where it is absorbed by plants, which are in turn eaten by fish.

4 On land the carbon dioxide gas is also taken in by plants which are then eaten by animals. Finally, people take in the radiocarbon when they eat fish, plants, and animals. In this way all living things continue to take in radiocarbon throughout their lives.

have decayed. After another 5,730 years, half of the remainder will have decayed.

Radiocarbon is therefore said to have a "half-life" of 5,730 years. If the original radiocarbon levels in an object made from once-living material, such as wood, are known and the radiocarbon level in the object today is measured, it should be possible to calculate how long the radiocarbon has been decaying and therefore how old the object is.

There are two ways of measuring the amount of radiocarbon in a sample. In one, a few grams of the material are needed. A second radiocarbon dating technique called Accelerator Mass Spectrometry (AMS), gives accurate results with only a few hundredths of a milligram of material. The tiny sample of material is separated out into all the different types of atoms that it is made from according to their mass, and the number of radiocarbon

atoms are then counted. Radiocarbon can date objects up to about 40,000 years old. Beyond that age, most of the radiocarbon has decayed and there is too little left to give an accurate result, but fortunately there are other techniques that will work with older objects. Radiocarbon dating is accurate to within 50-100 years for objects that are no older than 10,000 years. Dating accuracy becomes worse as the objects approach the test's limit of 40,000 years.

A whalebone casket from the eighth century. As it is made of a natural material, radiocarbon dating could be used to check if it was genuine.

HISTORY SPOTLIGHT

Radiocarbon dating was first suggested by Willard Libby, an American scientist, in the 1940s. But when it was used to date objects, it seemed to be producing the wrong dates. Sometimes, they were wrong by several centuries. The answer was that radiocarbon was not produced in the Earth's atmosphere at the same constant rate as scientists first assumed. Changes in the strength of the Earth's magnetic field and variations in the sun's activity both change the amount of radiocarbon in the atmosphere. These effects are now known and "radiocarbon dates" can now be corrected so that radiocarbon dating can give the age of an object to within 100 years and sometimes to within 20 years.

A scientist working with a mass spectrometer.

The remains of an ancient human body found in a bog. Radiocarbon dating could help to establish when the man was alive.

DATING BY LIGHT

A Greek vase showing Theseus killing the Minotaur. Pottery can now be dated by a technique called thermoluminescence.

Radiocarbon is a very useful way of dating objects, but of course it can only be applied to objects and materials that contain carbon. Fortunately, there are other methods that can be used with those materials that do not contain carbon. One of these other methods relies on detecting and measuring a mysterious light that some archaeological objects can be made to produce.

Fakes of ancient pottery can be very difficult indeed to spot. Fortunately, these objects can now be dated accurately by a technique called thermoluminescence, or TL.

The clay from which pottery is made contains tiny crystals of materials such as quartz. Radioactive elements present in the clay and especially in the ground around buried pottery decay in the same way as radiocarbon (see pages 38-39). The particles that fly out of the atoms when they decay strike atoms in the pottery and knock electrons out of them. These electrons travel through the pottery and become trapped in the quartz crystals. If the pottery is heated, the heat gives the trapped electrons enough energy to escape from their traps. Some of them release their excess energy as a tiny flash of light. This is thermoluminescence, meaning light produced by heating. The older a piece of pottery is, the more thermoluminescence it should produce. The processes involved are not fully understood, but TL seems to work well as a means of

A lake of lava in Zaire. One dating method relies on the fact that when volcanic rock is formed it contains no argon gas. But over the centuries, argon gas builds up in the rock. When the rock is analyzed, the amount of argon gas in it is used to calculate its age. And this in turn can be used to date objects found buried nearby.

dating objects with the right sort of crystalline structure.

But why does TL measure the age of the pottery and not the much greater age of the clay the pottery is made from? The answer lies in the way that pottery is made. Clay is very soft and easily modeled or molded to make figures, jars, and pots, but then it must be hardened. And this is done by baking it in a special oven called a kiln. The process is called firing. The high temperatures used to fire clay release all of the trapped electrons. The process of trapping electrons that will eventually produce thermoluminescence in the laboratory starts from scratch again after the clay is fired. So, when the TL test is performed, the thermoluminescence produced dates back only to when the clay was fired.

TL is a very useful technique for dating materials that do not contain any carbon, and therefore cannot be dated by the radiocarbon method, or are older than the 40,000-year limit for radiocarbon. It is probably correct to within about 10 percent of the age of the object. So, a 200,000-year-old object could produce a TL test result of 180,000 to 220,000 years.

Two other dating methods are worth mentioning – uranium-series dating and potassium-argon dating. Both of them rely on the fact that some elements are unstable and change slowly with time. When an element undergoes radioactive decay, it changes from the original element into new elements until it reaches a stable state. The chain of elements is well known. The amounts and types of elements in the decay chain found in the ground give an indication of the age of the deposit and anything that is buried in it.

How Old Is That Pot?

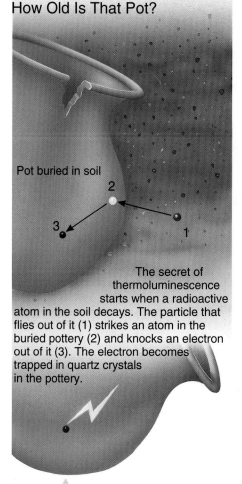

Pot buried in soil

The secret of thermoluminescence starts when a radioactive atom in the soil decays. The particle that flies out of it (1) strikes an atom in the buried pottery (2) and knocks an electron out of it (3). The electron becomes trapped in quartz crystals in the pottery.

Centuries later, when the pottery is heated in the laboratory, the electron escapes from its trap and emits a tiny flash of light.

Growth rings on a cross section of a coniferous tree.

COUNTING RINGS

It is well known that the age of a tree can be found by counting the rings across the trunk when the tree has been cut down. From this simple fact, scientists have developed a very accurate way of dating wooden objects that may be thousands of years old.

Bristlecone pines are among the oldest trees on Earth.

In the parts of the world that have cold winters and warm summers, most trees lie dormant during the winter and grow during the summer by adding a new ring of wood around their trunks. That is why old trees have thicker trunks than young trees. Good growing conditions produce thicker growth rings than poor conditions. As the weather and therefore the growing conditions vary from year to year, the thickness of the growth rings also varies. All the trees of the same species (oaks, for example) growing in the same part of the world experience the same weather conditions and so their ring patterns should also be the same.

The growth rings of a recently felled tree can be given dates as long as the year of felling is known. If the life span of an older tree overlaps the first tree, their ring patterns will also overlap. So, the rings of the older tree can be dated back to its first year. If progressively older trees with rings that overlap in the same way are added, the tree ring record can sometimes be extended back several thousand years into the past. Oaks in Ireland, for example, have provided a tree ring record 7,000 years old. If a wood carving or a timber from a dwelling, for example, is compared to this tree ring record, its ring pattern should match the record for the period when the tree was alive. If an object thought to be 1,000 years old matches the tree ring record from 500 years ago, it must be a fake.

Artists have sometimes used wood panels to paint on. If a painting thought to be 400 years old is painted on a wood panel shown by the tree ring record to be only 100 years old, then it must be a fake. Dating wooden objects in this way is called dendrochronology.

The record for one species of tree from one place, the Irish oaks for example, can only be used to date wood from the same species of tree from the same area. A piece of wood from somewhere else in the world, North America for example, could not be dated by means of this Irish oak record. Different species of trees must be used to date wooden objects from other places.

Dendrochronology's only major problem is that a large piece of wood, about 100 rings wide, is needed to date an unknown piece of wood with absolute certainty. Smaller pieces of wood can be dated, but with less certainty.

Dendrochronology has been helpful in confirming the results of other dating methods such as radiocarbon (see pages 38-39). An individual growth ring in a piece of wood can be dated by the radiocarbon it contains. If the two dates are not the same, it is the radiocarbon date that must be wrong. And therefore dendrochronology is used to help correct errors in the radiocarbon method.

Dendrochronology can be used to date buried wooden objects like this 16th-century boat in Holland.

A Spanish medieval painting of St. George and the dragon. The wooden panel on which it is painted could be used to help date the work of art.

GLOSSARY

arsenic A very poisonous element found in early copper.

brass An alloy of the elements copper and zinc.

bronze An alloy of the elements copper and tin.

counterfeit An imitation of a real object made to trick someone.

dendrochronology A method for dating wooden objects by means of the pattern of growth rings in the wood.

electron microscope A very powerful microscope capable of magnifying samples up to several hundred thousand times.

fake Something that is not real, or something made to look more valuable than it really is.

flint A hard, brittle, rocky material, mostly silica (sand), used by prehistoric people to make tools and weapons.

forgery Something (usually a document) made to cheat someone.

fraud The act of cheating or deceiving people to gain an advantage over them.

hallmark A mark pressed into valuable objects made from gold, silver, or platinum that shows the quality of the metal and the year in which the object was made.

hoax A trick designed to mislead people.

isotopes Different forms of an element which differ only in the number of neutrons in the nucleus at the center of their atoms, but have the same chemical properties.

microscopy The use of microscopes to enlarge a sample and study it in more detail.

potassium-argon dating A method for dating an object by measuring how much radioactive potassium has decayed to form argon.

radiocarbon An isotope of carbon.

radiocarbon dating Dating an object that was once alive by measuring the amount of radiocarbon it contains.

stable isotope analysis Identifying where a material comes from by measuring how much of each isotope of carbon and oxygen it contains.

thermoluminescence A method for dating pottery by measuring the amount of a special light caused by radioactive decay given out by the sample.

FURTHER READING

Arvey, Michael. *UFOs: Opposing Viewpoints.* Greenhaven, 1989

Barber, Jacqueline. *Crime Lab Chemistry.* Lawrence Science, 1989

Billings, Charlene W. *Lasers: The New Technology of Light.* Facts on File, 1992

Christian, Mary B. *Bigfoot.* Macmillan, 1987

Gonen, Rivka. *Fired Up! How Ancient Pottery Was Made.* Lerner, 1993

Grahm, Ian. *Lasers and Holograms.* Franklin Watts, 1991

Kolb, Kenneth, E., and Kolb, Doris K. *Glass: Its Many Facets.* Enslow, 1988

Landau, Elaine. *Yeti, Abominable Snowman of the Himalayas.* Millbrook, 1993

Liptak, Karen. *Dating Dinosaurs and other Old Things.* Millbrook, 1992

Rasmussen, Richard M. *The UFO Challenge.* Lucent Books, 1990

San Souci, Robert. *Loch Ness Monster: Opposing Viewpoints.* Greenhaven, 1989

Symes, R. F. and Harding, Roger. *Crystal and Gem.* Knopf, 1991

Tesar, Jenny. *Scientific Crime Investigation.* Franklin Watts, 1991

INDEX